CONTEMPORARY ART

★ IN MY GALLERY ★

WRITTEN BY
EMILIE DUFRESNE

DESIGNED BY
DANIELLE RIPPENGILL

BookLife
PUBLISHING

©2020
BookLife Publishing Ltd.
King's Lynn
Norfolk PE30 4LS

All rights reserved.
Printed in Malaysia.

A catalogue record for this book is available from the British Library.

ISBN: 978-1-78637-849-1

Written by:
Emilie Dufresne

Edited by:
Madeline Tyler

Designed by:
Danielle Rippengill

IMAGE CREDITS

COVER AND THROUGHOUT – ARTBESOURO, APRIL_PIE, SHTONADO, TASHANATASHA, QUARTA, PELONMAKER, ART4ALL, STREJMAN, JOHNJOHNSON, 19SRB81. BACKGROUNDS – EXPRESSVECTORS. HENRI & ARTISTS – GRINBOX. GALLERY – GOODSTUDIO, SIBERIAN ART. 2 – CRYSTAL EYE STUDIO, ANGYEE PATIPAT. 5 – FOCUS_BELL. 8 – ALIAKSEI KRUHLENIA. 9 – YULIYA DARAFEI, DELCARMAT. 10 – CINCINART, DREAM MASTER. 11 – ILKAYALPTEKIN. 14&15 – ANASTASIIA VLASOVA. 18&19 – LETOVSEGDA, YEKATERINALIM. 22&23 – FOCUS_BELL, VASIF MAHAROV. 26&27 – CRYSTAL EYE STUDIO, ANGYEE PATIPAT. 28&29 – ICON FONT ILLUSTRATION, MSPOINT, GRINBOX. IMAGES ARE COURTESY OF SHUTTERSTOCK.COM. WITH THANKS TO GETTY IMAGES, THINKSTOCK PHOTO AND ISTOCKPHOTO.

CONTENTS

Words that look like **this** are explained in the glossary on page 31.

WELCOME TO THE GALLERY

Hi! I'm Henri and I am an expert in Contemporary Art. I work in this gallery and I am going to teach you all about Contemporary Art and create some artworks with you as well. We need to be ready for opening night!

Museums and Galleries

Museums and galleries are very important to the world's **culture**. They look after and **exhibit** artworks to the public. We can learn a lot from art, such as people's thoughts and ideas, and what was happening in the world when the art was created.

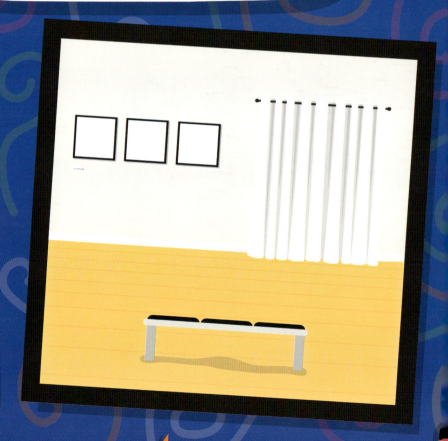

TYPES OF ART

There are so many different types of art in the world that I can't teach you about all of them. So, here are some of the ones we will be seeing in this book.

Performance art is a type of art that is often performed live in front of viewers or spectators. Sometimes the people watching must take part in the performance.

Installations are pieces of art that are installed in a gallery. The audience usually has to walk around or interact with the artwork in order to experience it, rather than just look at it.

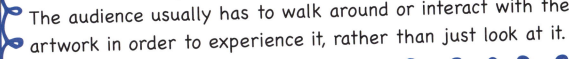

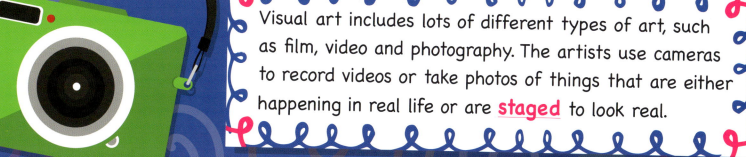

Visual art includes lots of different types of art, such as film, video and photography. The artists use cameras to record videos or take photos of things that are either happening in real life or are **staged** to look real.

CONTEMPORARY ART WING

Welcome to the Contemporary Art Wing. This wing is particularly big because we need to fit lots of different types of art in it! Let's see what types of art we will have and where everything is going to go.

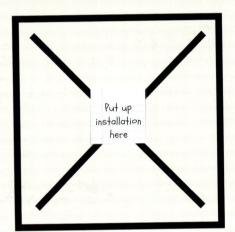

Put up installation here

Performance space here

A museum or gallery might have different floors or areas inside it. These areas might have different exhibitions from different artists or **movements**. This whole wing is going to be exhibiting Contemporary Art.

6

We could show the performance art in that corner, then have installations and photographs across the rest of the wing. There is a special material under this cloth we will use it to show art that isn't usually found in an art gallery.

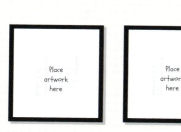

Place artwork here

Place artwork here

Place artwork here

Put up brick wall here

I can't wait for opening night – there is going to be so much going on in this wing!

OFTEN, INSTALLATIONS AND PERFORMANCE ARTWORKS TAKE UP A WHOLE ROOM OF A GALLERY. THIS LETS THE AUDIENCE IMMERSE THEMSELVES INTO THE PIECE.

WHAT IS CONTEMPORARY ART?

Big C, Little C

Contemporary Art can be a very confusing type of art to explain. This is because 'contemporary art' with a small 'c' means art that is being created now or has been made in your lifetime. However, 'Contemporary Art' with a capital 'C' is a **period** of art that began around the mid-1900s.

EXAMPLE OF YOUNG BRITISH ART

Now and Then

Contemporary Art has been around for many years. This means that inside the period of Contemporary Art there have been many different art movements. Some of these include **Pop Art**, **Young British Art** and **Computer Art**.

Before Contemporary Art

Before the period of Contemporary Art, there was a period called Modern Art. Modern Art began in the 1800s and marked a **significant** change in art. Artists in the Modern Art period stopped painting scenes from history and religion and began painting scenes from everyday life in new and exciting ways.

CUBIST ARTWORK

IMPRESSIONIST ARTWORK

More Modern

Artists in the Modern Art period also began using brighter colours, new materials and interesting techniques. Different Modern Art movements used different techniques. **Impressionists** used light colours, **Cubists** tried to show objects through shapes and **Post-Impressionists** showed how they were feeling through their **brushstrokes** and colours.

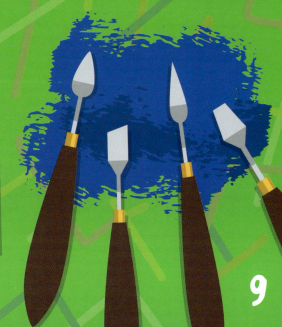

Out with the Old

Even though Modern Art was seen as very **revolutionary** when it started, by the end of the 1800s, artists were doing more and more interesting things and pushing art into newer and even more exciting places. Contemporary Art is known for how **diverse** it is and how many different types of art have come from it.

Technological Transformation

During the Contemporary Art period, lots of new technology has been created. Artists have used this new technology to create new art forms such as film, **digital art** and performance art.

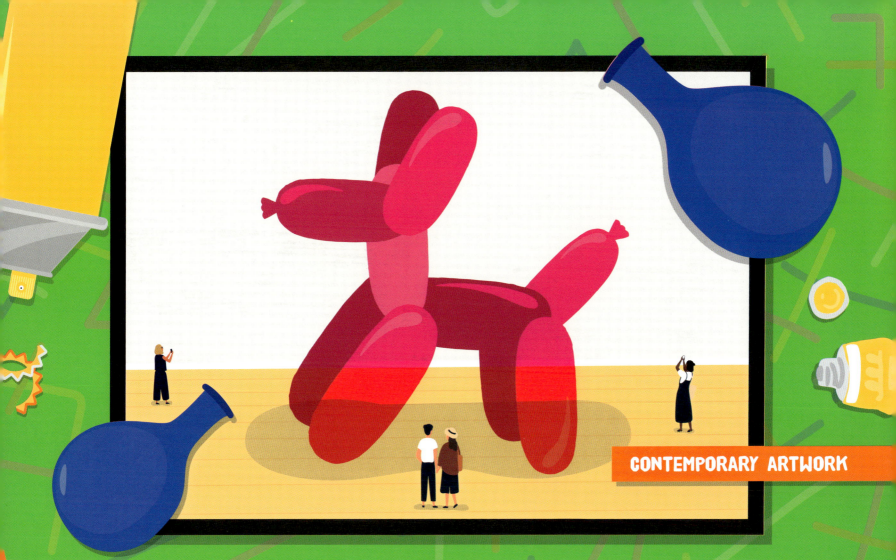

CONTEMPORARY ARTWORK

Constantly Questioning

It is hard to say what defines Contemporary Art because there are so many different movements within the period. Many Contemporary artists question what art is and what it could be. This is what makes it such a diverse and interesting period.

The World Is Yours

Throughout the Contemporary Art period, communication across the world has been getting better and better. This means it has become easier and easier for people to share ideas and techniques. This helped art to become more and more diverse.

MARINA ABRAMOVIĆ

Country of Birth: Serbia (former Yugoslavia)
Born: 1946

Marina Abramović is seen as a leader in performance art. She was part of a group of artists in the 1970s who began experimenting with live performance as a form of art. She is known for pushing her mind and body to the limit in her performances. Her performances included ideas of **endurance** and pain. At an exhibition of Abramović's work in the Museum of Modern Art in New York, she performed a piece called *The Artist Is Present*. During this performance, Abramović sat in a chair for eight hours every day for three months and invited people to sit opposite her. They would then stare into each other's eyes in front of everyone for as long as the visitor wanted to.

Abramović also changed the roles between the artist and the viewer in some of her artworks. Instead of using a canvas, Abramović made her own body the place where art could be created, and often people would become the artists in her performance pieces.

Activity:
PART OF THE PERFORMANCE

You will need:

- Old, white-coloured clothes ☑
- Felt tip pens in different colours ☑
- Face paint in different colours ☑
- Crayons in different colours ☑
- Sponges ☑
- Paintbrushes ☑
- A table and tablecloth ☑
- A chair ☑

Grab some old clothes and paints – you are about to become the canvas, just like Abramović!

Make sure you get a grown-up to help you choose materials that you know are safe for your skin.

First, you need to make sure the tablecloth is on the table and there is nothing around you or on the floor – this could get messy. Ask a grown-up to make sure everything is paint-proof before the performance starts.

Now you need to arrange all your materials on the table. Next, change into your old, white-coloured clothes.

Invite your friends, family, or people you live with to be part of the performance. Tell them that they can paint and draw whatever they want on you.

Sit in the chair and be the canvas while the people you know paint on you and your clothes. Now you are the artwork!

ANISH KAPOOR

Country of Birth: India
Born: 1954

Anish Kapoor is an artist who is mostly known for his **sculptures** and installations. His artworks make the viewer think about themselves and how they fit into the world around them. He does this by using special materials to make his sculptures. These materials might be a **reflective** metal or the blackest of black paints.

In his work *Cloud Gate*, Kapoor created a large, bean-shaped sculpture out of metal. The reflective and curved shape means that when people look at the sculpture, they see themselves, the sky and the city all at once. This makes people think about where they fit in the world around them.

Kapoor is also known for using a very **pigmented** black paint. In Kapoor's work *Descent into Limbo*, he created a large hole in a gallery floor and painted it with this black paint. It made the hole look like a flat surface on the ground. This made people question whether what they were seeing was real or not, and what the artwork meant.

Activity:

INFINITY INSTALLATION

You will need:

The blackest paint you have ☑

White paint ☑

Paintbrushes ☑

Large sheets of thick card ☑

Scissors ☑

Aluminium foil ☑

PVA glue ☑

Sticky tape ☑

A large cardboard box ☑

We are going to make two different infinity sculptures to install in the gallery.

For the first part of this piece, cut out a big circle from a sheet of card. Paint it black – don't forget the edges! Let it dry, ready to be put on the floor later.

Now for the second part – the reflective piece. Paint the cardboard box white all over and leave it to dry. Take a large rectangular piece of card and glue sheets of aluminium foil over it. Now bend it into a cone shape with the foil inside, and fasten it with sticky tape.

Cut a circular hole in the bottom of the box the same size as the wide part of the cone. Cover the outside of the hole in aluminium foil as well. Stick the cone inside the hole so that the wide opening points outwards. Next, put the box against a wall so that nobody can see the cone.

SHIRIN NESHAT

Country of Birth: Iran
Born: 1957

Shirin Neshat is a visual artist who works mostly with video, film and photography. She was originally born in Iran and then moved to the US to study art.

Her artworks discuss very important and **political** themes such as **identity**, **gender**, culture and religion. Her art is seen as very political because it makes people think about how different countries are run and how people see their own culture.

Her artworks often explore the changes she has seen in her birth country of Iran. In many of her works, she tries to tell the stories and experiences of women in Iran. For example, she created a series of black and white photographs of herself in Iranian dress. She then wrote lines from religious texts over her hands, feet and face. This explored how women saw their identity in Iran at the time.

Activity:
PHOTOGRAPHY FOR EXPLORATION

You will need:

A camera ☑

A printer ☑

Permanent markers ☑

We are going to try to explore our identities and culture through photography, just like Neshat. Grab your camera!

Before we can create any photography, you need to think about your identity and culture.

First, think about your past, such as the place where you were born, your favourite books or toys from when you were younger, or anything that you feel makes up your identity. I have chosen this bear that I have had all my life.

Once you have your idea, it is time to take your photo. I am going to take mine in black and white like Neshat did, but you could use any colours or effects for your photos.

Now print off the picture and use the permanent markers to write some of your favourite lines from books and films that you used to like when you were younger.

BANKSY

Banksy is an anonymous artist. This means that nobody knows who Banksy is. He is most famous for his graffiti and street art. Graffiti is art that is done on the sides of buildings or in public places using spray paint. Graffiti art is mostly against the law, but since Banksy has gained fame, his works are celebrated, where another graffiti artist would be **prosecuted**. Banksy is known for using stencils to create his pieces. He has painted buildings and walls across the world and is known for making people think about politics through funny and thought-provoking artwork.

Now his fame is so great, his artworks are seen as very important and if a work is created on the wall of a building, the wall is sometimes removed so that the artwork can be sold and shown in art galleries.

Banksy's artworks often make people question what is and isn't art and why people think some artforms are better, or more skillful, than others.

Activity:
STENCILS AND SPRAY PAINTS

You will need:

Sheets of thick paper and card ☑

Scissors ☑

Letter stencils ☑

Pencils ☑

Spray paints in different colours ☑

A dust or paint mask ☑

It's time to create some street art, just like Banksy!

Always have a grown-up with you when using scissors and don't forget to wear your dust mask when spray painting.

First, you need to think about what you want your stencil to show. Think about sayings or phrases that you hear a lot. I have gone with 'grow up' – I get told to do that a lot.

Use your letter stencil to write out the words on one piece of paper. On a different piece of paper, draw the outline of the picture you want – I have chosen a child and a very long rectangular shape. Now cut out the stencils and choose which colours you want each stencil to be.

Place one of your stencils onto the card you want your graffiti to be displayed on. Then spray one colour over the stencil. Place and spray each stencil separately. Only spray one colour on each stencil so that they don't mix. Let your picture dry and there you have it – your very own graffiti artwork.

OPENING NIGHT

Wow! The wing looks great now that all the installations and photographs are up and the performance piece has started. Let's see what people are saying.

Talking about art is important. Thinking about how art makes us feel can help us to understand an artwork and ourselves better. Which of the pieces you created do you like the most and why? How do these pieces make you feel?

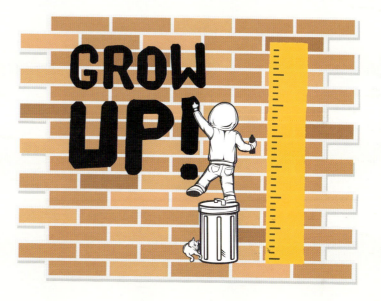

Why do you think the words are in colour and the photographs are in black and white?

It feels like the places are harder to remember than the words to me.

I don't like it... Why would someone take street art away from the street?

I love that this one is on a brick wall!

QUIZ

1. Which art period came before Contemporary Art?

2. Can you name three art movements within the Contemporary Art period?

3. Which artist is known for her performance artworks that test her body and mind?

4. What three types of art does Shirin Neshat work with most?

5. Which anonymous artist creates street art using stencils?

Answers: 1. Modern Art **2.** Pop Art, Young British Art and Computer Art **3.** Marina Abramović **4.** Photography, video and film **5.** Banksy

Have you ever been to a museum or gallery?

Visiting museums and galleries can teach us about different artists, movements and types of art. You can always try to create art in the style of the people you see. Don't forget to talk about the art you see and how it makes you feel.

We want to see your artworks! If you do any of the activities in this book, why not put it on social media and use #InMyGalleryContemporaryArt so that we can see what you have created.

GLOSSARY

brushstrokes	the different marks made with paintbrushes onto a surface
Computer Art	art made or shown using the digital technology of computers
Cubists	artists belonging to an art movement in which people and objects were represented through geometric shapes such as cubes
culture	the traditions, ideas and ways of life of a particular group of people
digital art	art that uses digital technology such as computers, videos and televisions
diverse	having many different kinds or types
endurance	being able to do something that is mentally or physically tiring for a long time
exhibit	to show art
gender	the different roles and stereotypes that a society or culture gives to the different sexes
identity	the things that make a particular person, group or place different from others
immerse	to be completely involved
Impressionists	artists belonging to an art movement that aimed to give the impression of movement through light and colour
movements	categories or types of art that an artwork or artist might belong to, which can sometimes be related to a certain time or place
period	a long period of time that may include many different art movements
pigmented	having a strong colour
political	relating to things that are about politics
Pop Art	an art movement that was heavily influenced by things in popular culture such as celebrities, adverts and comics
Post-Impressionists	artists belonging to an art movement that pushed the ideas of Impressionism even further, using light, colour and expression in their paintings
prosecuted	to have charged someone with a crime
reflective	able to bounce back colour and light like a mirror
revolutionary	doing something in a way that drastically changes how it was done or thought of before
sculptures	decorative objects made through carving, chiselling or moulding
significant	to be important or noteworthy
staged	put together or performed in a certain way
Young British Art	an art movement made up of young artists living and working in Britain

INDEX